D0622653

DISCARD

What Is Panic Disorder?

Other titles in the *Understanding Mental Disorders* series include:

What Is Panic Disorder?

Carla Mooney

ReferencePoint
Press®

San Diego, CA

© 2016 ReferencePoint Press, Inc.
Printed in the United States

For more information, contact:
ReferencePoint Press, Inc.
PO Box 27779
San Diego, CA 92198
www.ReferencePointPress.com

LIBRARY OF CONGRESS CATALOGING-IN-PUBLICATION DATA

Mooney, Carla, 1970-
    What is panic disorder?/by Carla Mooney.
        pages cm. -- (Understanding mental disorders)
    Audience: Grade 9 to 12.
    Includes bibliographical references and index.
    ISBN-13: 978-1-60152-924-4 (hardback)
    ISBN-10: 1-60152-924-4 (hardback)
    1. Panic disorders--Juvenile literature. I. Title.
RC535.M63 2016
616.85'223--dc23
                                                         2015016553

CONTENTS

INTRODUCTION

Sudden Terror

One evening, Lee Kynaston went out to dinner with friends. He ordered his food and was about to begin eating when he was quickly overwhelmed with panic. He remembers how quickly the terror struck, saying:

> One minute I was in a restaurant with friends about to tuck into a bowl of spaghetti; the next I was on the street outside, crouched by a bin bag, hyperventilating, sweating and trembling uncontrollably. Gripped by a sudden, irrational fear (of what, I still don't know) and overwhelmed by adrenaline, I had fled the restaurant so quickly that my friends suspected I had been violently sick. All I knew is that I had to flee.[1]

Once outside the restaurant, Kynaston was dizzy and disoriented. He struggled to breathe, and his heart raced. As people outside the restaurant stared at him, he was certain that he was dying.

At the time Kynaston did not recognize that he was having a panic attack. After calming down and returning home, he rationalized his reaction as tiredness, stress, or an adverse reaction to something he had eaten or drunk. He assumed that the incident was an isolated, one-time event.

Yet over the next few weeks, the panic attacks returned. With each attack, Kynaston began to fear them more, which caused his symptoms to intensify. "They would happen randomly: sometimes in the street, sometimes while I was in the house getting ready to go out or, like the first one and most inconveniently of all, in the middle of meals,"[2] he says. Going to work became a problem because Kynaston feared having another panic attack while riding public transportation. Many times he would get on the subway and then have to get off a stop or two later because his fear became too intense. He began to stay home to avoid having an attack in public. For nearly six months he refused to eat in a restaurant, afraid that he would have another attack in the middle of a meal.

After months of attacks, the tightness in his chest became so intense that Kynaston was convinced that he was having a heart attack. He went to the hospital, afraid that he was going to die. After examining him, the doctor explained to Kynaston that he was not having a heart attack and was in no danger of immediate death. So Kynaston went to see a mental health professional, who diagnosed him with panic disorder.

When Fear Is Real

Panic disorder is a serious mental illness, part of a group of mental illnesses called anxiety disorders. Fear and anxiety are normal emotions. But when anxiety does not go away and gets worse over time, a person may have an anxiety disorder. Some people with anxiety disorder experience panic attacks, like Kynaston. These attacks can feature chest pain, dizziness, and trouble breathing. People with panic disorder have repeated attacks of severe anxiety or fear that can last for several minutes or even longer. These feelings are so intense that the person may feel as if he or she is going to die or a disaster is about to occur. Sometimes anxiety and panic attacks get so bad that they interfere with a person's ability to lead a normal life.

> "They would happen randomly: sometimes in the street, sometimes while I was in the house getting ready to go out or, like the first one and most inconveniently of all, in the middle of meals."[2]
>
> —Lee Kynaston, a panic disorder sufferer.

People who have never suffered a full-blown panic attack may have trouble understanding the extent to which it can disable a person. In fact, in today's society the term *panic attack* is sometimes thrown around loosely, and some people may exaggerate the general anxiety that is normal to feel by describing themselves as having a panic attack. However, author Priscilla

Stepping onto a crowded New York City subway train (pictured) is enough to spark panic in someone with panic disorder. People with this disorder sometimes hide in their homes to avoid having a panic attack in public.

Warner says there is a huge difference between feeling reasonable, moderate, and appropriate anxiety and fear and experiencing the sensory and seemingly life-threating assault that characterizes having a panic attack. When she first started having panic attacks at age fifteen, "that phrase hadn't even been invented," she says. "Now people use it to describe anything from a major health crisis to the inability to buy their favorite shoes at a sample sale. To those of us who suffer from terrifying physical symptoms, that both minimizes our experience and confuses us. Is what we are suffering from real? Is panic a figment of our imagination?"[3]

Rita Zoey Chin is another person who can testify to the terror invoked by panic disorder. She suffered for years, and her disorder all but took over her life. Chin explains:

My panic attacks proliferated like mice. I simply woke up one day, infested. I began to fear things I didn't know were possible to fear: open spaces, small spaces, heat, crossing a street. I panicked in the shower, in the car, in the grocery store, for no apparent reason—each time feeling slightly more battered than the last. When I wasn't panicking, I was worrying about all the grisly calamities that can befall a person. *A plane will crash into the living room. You will choke on a bite of sandwich. A mosquito will infect you with Eastern equine encephalitis virus.* Even going upstairs to make the bed or taking a shower by myself became insurmountable. So I planned my showers for when Larry [her husband] was home. I avoided the stairs as much as possible. I stopped driving on the highway. My life was overrun.[4]

Millions of Sufferers

People with panic disorder are not alone—the Anxiety and Depression Association of America (ADAA) estimates that approximately 6 million adults in the United States suffer from panic disorder.

Panic disorder can affect anyone, rich or poor, young or old. Many prominent Americans have suffered from panic disorder. For example, sufferers count among themselves Emma Stone—an outgoing actress who has starred in action films, dramas, and comedies. As a child, however, Stone experienced terrible panic attacks that prevented her from socializing with others. "I was just kind of immobilized by it," she says of the attacks, which began when she was eight years old. "I didn't want to go to my friends' houses or hang out with anybody, and nobody really understood."[5] Other celebrities who have suffered from panic attacks include singer Ellie Goulding, television reporter Dan Harris, and Pro Football Hall of Fame running back Earl Campbell.

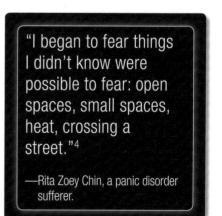

"I began to fear things I didn't know were possible to fear: open spaces, small spaces, heat, crossing a street."[4]

—Rita Zoey Chin, a panic disorder sufferer.

There is hope for people diagnosed with panic disorder. Kynaston saw a mental health therapist to treat his illness. In therapy, he learned to identify his irrational thoughts and interrupt the cycle of anxiety, panic, and fear. He credits therapy with helping him control his panic attacks. "Since my therapy I have had just one single attack which was mild," he reports. "Instead of seeing it as a life-threating incident I dismissed it as an annoyance."[6] With treatment, patients can learn to manage the disorder and regain control over their lives.

CHAPTER 1

What Is Panic Disorder?

Fear and anxiety are the body's natural response to danger. When a person feels threatened, it triggers a physical reaction called the fight-or-flight response. This innate reaction activates certain areas of the brain that release chemicals to increase heart rate, blood pressure, and breathing rate. These physical changes are designed to ensure survival by preparing the body to either fight or flee imminent danger. The fear response can help a person stay focused or leap into action.

For some people the fight-or-flight response can be triggered by false alarms, situations in which there is no real threat. Panic attacks are the reaction to these false alarms. People with panic disorder experience these sudden and repeated attacks of fear, even when no real danger is present. Their fear has a strong physical component; they experience chest pains, have trouble breathing, or feel weak and dizzy. The attacks may occur suddenly and at any time. For some the panic attacks become debilitating and interfere with work, school, activities, and relationships. Worried that they will have another panic attack, some may withdraw from family and friends. For these people, panic can become a serious mental illness.

Panic Attack Symptoms

Panic attacks are the main symptom of panic disorder. Sometimes these episodes can be triggered by a specific situation such as flying or being in a large group of people. In many cases, however, panic attacks strike without warning. They can develop at any time or place and are not tied to a specific object, event, or situation.

Panic attack symptoms usually peak within ten minutes, although in some cases they can last almost an hour. This occurs because the body cannot sustain the fight-or-flight response for a longer period without becoming exhausted. During a panic attack physical and emotional symptoms often increase in waves and then slowly subside. After the initial attack ends, a person may still feel anxious and jittery for many hours.

Sufferers usually feel helpless to stop an attack. During the attack individuals may feel intense terror or fear. They may have heart palpitations and chest pain so severe they think they are having a heart attack. Others have trouble breathing, hyperventilate, or feel like they are choking. Individuals may experience hot flashes or chills. They may sweat profusely, tremble, or feel as if they are going to throw up. Some feel dizzy and light-headed, as if they are going to faint. Many people mistake these physical symptoms for another medical condition or illness, which may prompt them to visit a doctor. Once the doctor rules out a physical cause for their symptoms, they may be diagnosed as having a panic attack. To be diagnosed with a panic attack, a person must experience four or more symptoms at the same time. The symptoms must have developed abruptly and peaked within ten minutes of beginning.

Jemma Kidd, a makeup artist and writer from England who has panic disorder, experienced her first panic attack around age twenty, when she woke up with an inexplicably strange feeling. Throughout the day she felt increasingly detached from her surroundings and out of place. "It was weird—I was on familiar territory, surrounded by people I loved, but I couldn't help feeling frightened," she remembers. Then a few hours later, panic descended at full force. "Everything suddenly looked distorted. I felt sick, my heart began racing and I couldn't breathe. Within ten minutes it was over, but afterwards I felt as if I had been in a war zone."[7] In addition to feeling blindsided by the attack, Kidd was disturbed that she could not pinpoint its cause. Nothing bad or unusual had happened to explain the terror; nothing had gone awry or could otherwise explain the pet-

> "Everything suddenly looked distorted. I felt sick, my heart began racing and I couldn't breathe. Within ten minutes it was over, but afterwards I felt as if I had been in a war zone."[7]
>
> —Jemma Kidd, a panic disorder sufferer.

Panic attacks tend to come on suddenly, without warning. They can occur anytime and anyplace—when a person is at work, at home, on the train, or at the mall. Symptoms usually peak within minutes, although sufferers may feel tired and worn out after the attack subsides.

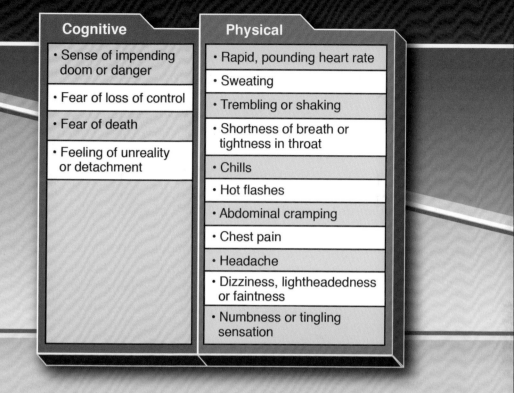

Cognitive	Physical
• Sense of impending doom or danger	• Rapid, pounding heart rate
• Fear of loss of control	• Sweating
• Fear of death	• Trembling or shaking
• Feeling of unreality or detachment	• Shortness of breath or tightness in throat
	• Chills
	• Hot flashes
	• Abdominal cramping
	• Chest pain
	• Headache
	• Dizziness, lightheadedness or faintness
	• Numbness or tingling sensation

Source: The Mayo Clinic, "Panic Attacks and Panic Disorder—Symptoms." www.mayoclinic.org.

rifying feelings that shook her to her core. Even worse, a few days later another panic attack struck, this time while she was driving. "I pulled over, disorientated and sweating, gasping for breath and with my heart palpitating. Again it was over within a few minutes, but I had no idea what was happening to me,"[8] she says.

The frequency of panic attacks varies from person to person. Some people experience attacks weekly over a period of months. Others experience attacks in daily clusters, with periods of remission that can last for weeks, months, or years. "I had panic attacks, sometimes daily, sometimes 10 times a day, sometimes only once a week,"[9] says Lisa T. McElroy, an associate professor of law at the Drexel University Earle Mack School of Law.

Panic Attack Versus Panic Disorder

Not everyone who has a panic attack goes on to develop panic disorder. Many people experience a panic attack or two during their lifetime and never have another. Panic attacks can also be a symptom of several other psychiatric disorders, such as obsessive-compulsive disorder (an anxiety disorder characterized by unreasonable thoughts or fears, called obsessions, that compel a person to perform certain repetitive behaviors, called rituals). They can also be due to having a specific phobia (an irrational fear of a particular object or situation). In fact, many people who have a mental illness (of which there are more than two hundred classified forms, according to the *Diagnostic and Statistical Manual of Mental Disorders*, the standard classification of mental disorders used by mental health professionals) will have at least one panic attack in their lifetime.

About 10 to 15 percent of American adults experience occasional panic attacks, and about 2 percent develop panic disorder. "A persistent heavy burden and lots of stress can trigger a panic attack, but one or a few of these attacks don't automatically lead to panic disorder," says researcher and psychologist Anders Hovland. "Panic disorder is characterized by repeated attacks and worries about being stricken by new ones,"[10] he says.

"Panic disorder is characterized by repeated attacks and worries about being stricken by new ones."[10]

—Anders Hovland, a researcher and psychologist.

In an attempt to avoid future panic attacks, people with recurring panic attacks may significantly change their behavior. They may avoid places and situations where attacks occurred in the past, which can include public transportation, restaurants, sporting events, and parties with family and friends. Avoiding so many common places disrupts individuals' ability to live a normal life and may signal they have developed full-blown panic disorder.

In order to be diagnosed with panic disorder, a person must have recurring panic attacks, experience excessive anxiety over future at-

Panic Disorder and Elderly Patients

Patients who are sixty-five or older may experience panic disorder differently than younger patients. Elderly patients with panic disorder are more likely to report physical symptoms such as trembling and sweating than psychological symptoms such as a fear of imminent death. Many elderly patients may hide their symptoms because they fear it will appear as if their mental abilities are in decline. Panic attacks can be brought on by underlying depression and anxiety over the loss of a partner, feelings of isolation, and failing health.

Because elderly patients are more likely to have other health problems for which they may be taking medication, the sudden appearance of panic attacks in a person who has not had them in the past can signal there is an underlying medical or medication problem. For example, changing medication doses or switching medications can sometimes trigger panic attack symptoms. In addition, as people age, common health problems such as heart disease or lung function can lead to anxiety, which may result in panic attacks. For these reasons, an elderly patient who complains of panic attacks should receive a full medical evaluation to rule out any other physical explanations.

tacks, and make significant behavioral changes as a result of the attacks. If any one of these conditions is not met, the person probably does not have panic disorder but another condition that features panic attacks as a symptom.

Anticipatory Anxiety and Avoidance

The memory of the fear and terror felt during a panic attack can negatively affect a person's emotional state and everyday life. Because having an attack makes a person feel so out of control, they tend to become extremely anxious about where and when the next panic attack will strike. "When I wasn't panicking, I panicked that I would start panicking," says McElroy. "I panicked that someone would find out that I was panicking. I panicked that the rest of my life would be a constant state of panic. I panicked that I would never have a career, or a family, or a regular home outside of a hospital."[11] Thinking about the possibility of another panic attack triggers what is called anticipatory anxiety. This condition can cause individuals to avoid people and places; their goal becomes to be alone, rather than in a public place, should a panic attack occur.

People who become anxious about panic attacks believe that if they avoid the place where a previous panic attack took place, they might be able to prevent future attacks. Over time they start avoiding more and more places. Avoidance may temporarily relieve anxiety over the fear of another attack, but it can make it nearly impossible for a person to lead a normal life. Sufferers may find themselves avoiding public places, events with friends, crowds, and other activities that they enjoyed in the past. After having a panic attack while driving on a highway, Traci Neal says that she changed her entire routine to avoid similar roads. "I rerouted my commute, declined invitations, stopped visiting friends and family, and asked others for rides to avoid having to drive on the highway,"[12] she says. However, such avoidance does not stop future panic attacks.

Agoraphobia

In some extreme cases of panic disorder, a person's avoidance of places and situations may lead to agoraphobia, a fear of public places and open spaces. People with agoraphobia become anxious in situations where they feel they cannot escape if a panic attack were to strike. They may become anxious in unfamiliar environments or places where they feel out of control and trapped, such as crowds or open spaces. They may also avoid traveling in a car, bus, or airplane.

According to the University of Pennsylvania's Perelman School of Medicine, about one of every three people with panic disorder develops agoraphobia. Becky, who lives in England, says that her agoraphobia developed after several years of intense anxiety and panic attacks. "It used to be that when I experienced a panic attack I would race outside for air, for distraction from my thoughts and feelings and to escape the almost claustrophobic sensations that I suffered," she says. But one day she felt faint and sick while outside, and she realized she had developed agoraphobia on top of panic disorder. "My biggest fear was that I would collapse in the street, all alone and that I wouldn't be able to get to safety,"[13] she says. According to the Univer-

People with panic disorder often change their behavior in hopes of preventing panic attacks. They might not go to public places, such as restaurants or movie theaters, or events, such as a football game or party.

sity of Chicago Medicine, approximately 1.8 million American adults will experience agoraphobia during any given year. Many develop agoraphobia after suffering one or more panic attacks.

Some people with agoraphobia will leave home occasionally, but only in the company of a friend or family member. In severe cases a person with agoraphobia may not leave his or her home for weeks, months, or even years, and doing so can trigger extreme anxiety and possibly a panic attack. This behavior can cause significant problems in relationships with family, friends, and partners.

For some people agoraphobia can last years. Australian Donna Bolton says that she has struggled with severe agoraphobia for about thirty-five years. For the past sixteen of them, she has largely confined herself to her home. "It's panic, you sweat, you're weak in the legs, you feel sick in the stomach, it's like you lose control of your whole body,"

Celebrities with Panic Disorder

According to Calm Clinic, a website by and for people with panic and anxiety disorders, many successful actors, writers, musicians, scientists, and celebrities have been diagnosed with and treated for panic attacks and panic disorder. These include the late princess Diana, singer David Bowie, actress and media mogul Oprah Winfrey, actor Johnny Depp, author John Steinbeck, physician Sigmund Freud, Norwegian painter Edvard Munch, actress Scarlett Johansson, singer Adele, and scientist Nikola Tesla.

says Bolton of how it feels to leave her house. "You'd wet your pants even. And you shake, you can't stop shaking."[14] Bolton's agoraphobia currently prevents her from having a job, and she says that it has been very hard on her children.

Who Is at Risk?

Anxiety disorders, including panic disorder, are the most common mental illnesses in the United States. According to the National Institute of Mental Health (NIMH), anxiety disorders affect about 40 million American adults ages eighteen and older in any given year—about 18 percent of the population. According to the ADAA, panic disorder affects about 6 million American adults.

Panic disorder can strike people of any age, gender, race, or socioeconomic background. However, some risk factors make a person have a greater chance of developing it. According to the ADAA, women are about twice as likely to develop panic disorder over their lifetime as men. Age is also a risk factor for developing panic disorder, which usually first strikes during late adolescence and early adulthood. According to the Perelman School of Medicine, about half of those who have panic disorder develop it before age twenty-four. In addition, older women may have a higher risk of panic disorder; studies have shown that panic attacks are common for women after menopause. Often the attacks are associated with stressful life events or health problems. Finally, the risk of developing panic disorder appears to be inherited. People who have close family members, such as parents or siblings, with panic disorder are more likely to be diagnosed with the disorder themselves.

Panic Disorder in Children and Teens

At one time panic disorder was believed to be strictly an adult disorder. However, studies have shown that many adults with panic disorder report that they had their first panic attack before age twenty. According to the NIMH, approximately 2.3 percent of thirteen- to eighteen-year-olds will experience panic disorder. Girls are more likely than boys to develop it. The risk of the disorder also increases with age—those who are seventeen to eighteen years old are more likely than thirteen- and fourteen-year-olds to develop it.

Panic disorder symptoms can be slightly different in children and teens than in adults. Children are more likely to report the physical symptoms of a panic attack—such as increased heart rate or trouble breathing—than the psychological symptoms (fear and loss of control).

The nature of being young can make children's panic disorder confusing for adult caretakers. A child having a panic attack may appear to be frightened or

> "It's panic, you sweat, you're weak in the legs, you feel sick in the stomach, it's like you lose control of your whole body."[14]
>
> —Donna Bolton, a panic disorder sufferer and agoraphobic.

upset with no identifiable cause, which can be challenging for parents. Very young children may not be able to adequately describe the feelings or fears that they experience during a panic attack. "When my son has a panic attack, he seems to be incapable of speech and his scream is high-pitched and sharp, like in a horror movie," says Karen Wang, the mother of a child who experiences panic attacks caused by agoraphobia. "His eyes are wide with fear. He starts hyperventilating and trembling right away. He will either try to run away or fight."[15] Older children and teens are usually better able to describe what happened during an attack once it has ended.

It is important to note that not all experiences of panic indicate the presence of panic disorder in a child. During a child's development, there are normal periods of anxiety. Many young children feel anxious over being separated from their parents or caregivers. They may throw tantrums, cry, or appear very worried. "Separation anxiety varies widely between children," says pediatrician Wendy Sue Swanson. "Some babies become hysterical when mom is out of sight for a very short time, while other children seem to demonstrate ongoing anxiety at separations during infancy, toddlerhood, and preschool."[16] Yet Swanson reassures parents that even though it can be unsettling, this behavior is normal and a sign of a meaningful attachment between parent and child. For most children this behavior will decrease with age. It is also normal for children to be afraid of a variety of ani-

Agoraphobia is the fear of public places and open spaces. The cabin of a commercial airliner might cause a person with this condition to feel trapped or out of control.

mals, strange situations, and objects. Lots of kids are afraid of the dark or dogs, even to the point of panic. These normal fears will generally ease as the child grows up.

Like adults, children's panic attacks are unpredictable, and many children with panic disorder will have attacks in school. Students with panic disorder may repeatedly and suddenly stop activities without an explanation. They may have difficulty concentrating, completing assignments, and following directions. They may attempt to hide their attacks from classmates and teachers and can be hesitant to describe their symptoms to teachers. They may not want to go to school or spend time with other children. They may also display low self-confidence at school and in social situations.

Ashley Nessman is one student who has struggled with anxiety since she was thirteen years old. She remembers what it felt like to have a panic attack in school, and she describes one particular attack that struck during midterm exams:

"When my son has a panic attack, he seems to be incapable of speech and his scream is high-pitched and sharp, like in a horror movie."[15]

—Karen Wang, whose child experiences panic attacks.

> The teacher had just placed the exam on my desk, I went to start writing my name, when suddenly I went numb. I felt paralyzed. I was sweating profusely, I started to tremble and shiver uncontrollably, my face turned red, I felt light-headed, and I ending up slipping out of my desk down to the floor. I was still conscious, but I couldn't make words. . . . After a few minutes (that felt like an eternity) I was able to catch my breath and come down from the panic attack.[17]

Untreated, panic disorder can have a significant effect on a child's life. Relationships with peers and family may suffer, and children with untreated panic disorder may have trouble academically. Such children are also at risk of developing depression or another mental illness. In some extreme cases the child may think about harming him- or herself or wanting to die.

High school student Nadia Mastroianni from Ontario, Canada, says that she began to experience daily panic attacks when she started ninth grade. With each attack, she experienced profuse sweating, a racing heartbeat, nausea, and a detached feeling. "It felt like I was dying," she says. "I was confused and petrified that this was happening."[18]

Although Mastroianni talked to some of her friends about what was happening to her, she tried to hide her symptoms from her parents and teachers. "I didn't know what was going on with my body," she says. Her parents had a hard time understanding what she was going through. "I think at one point they attributed it to typical teenage behavior, but when you don't know yourself what's wrong, it's really hard to explain it to others," she says. At one point Mastroianni's anxiety and fear overwhelmed her so much that she stayed in bed for about six weeks. She fell behind in school, which further added to her stress. "I was scared to face my teachers,"[19] she says. As time went on, the attacks continued to the point that Mastroianni no longer wanted to hang out with her friends and could not leave her house without feeling scared. Finally, in January 2014 Mastroianni admitted herself to the hospital, where she was diagnosed with panic disorder.

Coexisting Medical Conditions

Panic disorder commonly occurs along with other mental or physical illnesses. In many cases these illnesses mask the symptoms of panic disorder and need to be treated before a panic disorder treatment can be successful. Medical conditions that commonly occur along with panic disorder include cardiac arrhythmias, hyperthyroidism, asthma, chronic obstructive pulmonary disease, and irritable bowel syndrome.

Other anxiety disorders are also commonly present with panic disorder, including generalized anxiety disorder, social phobias, specific phobias, and obsessive-compulsive disorder. Someone with panic disorder may very well be diagnosed with another mental disorder too. When more than one disorder or disease is diagnosed in the same person, the disorders are called comorbid. Anxiety disorders like panic disorder are often comorbid with mood disorders such as depression and bipolar disorder. Having comorbid disorders can make treatment more complicated. The presence of each disorder may affect and worsen the symptoms of the other. Sometimes the symptoms of each disorder mirror each other, making it difficult to get a correct diagnosis.

People with panic disorder may experience the symptoms of other conditions, even without being diagnosed with them. For example, a person with panic disorder may become depressed about the ways the disorder has affected his or her life. This does not necessarily mean that the person also has depression; rather, the person is experiencing depressive symptoms in reaction to his or her panic disorder.

A Serious Medical Condition

Many people with panic disorder are embarrassed to admit that they have a problem. As a result, they may try to hide their fears and symptoms from others. However, panic disorder can be a serious medical condition, and without treatment, it can last for years. Untreated panic disorder can also lead to depression, phobias, substance abuse, and other medical and psychological problems. In extreme cases a person with panic disorder may consider suicide as a way to escape from panic and anxiety. Finding the right treatment may take time but is clearly important.

CHAPTER 2

What Causes Panic Disorder?

Men and women of all ages, races, and socioeconomic backgrounds can develop panic disorder. The causes of this mental illness are not fully understood, which makes it difficult to predict with certainty who will develop it. Most mental health experts believe panic disorder is not caused by one specific factor, but instead by a combination of biological, genetic, psychological, and environmental factors.

The presence of one or more risk factors, however, does not guarantee a person will develop panic disorder; it only means they have an increased chance of doing so. Many people with risk factors for panic disorder never develop it, but the more risk factors a person has, the more likely he or she will become ill. Learning about panic disorder's risk factors can help a person determine whether he or she is vulnerable to the disorder, recognize the warning signs and symptoms, and understand possible treatments.

Gender

Women have twice the risk of developing panic disorder as men, though the reason why is unknown. Some doctors believe that the hormonal changes that women experience during certain periods in their lives increase their risk. Panic attacks tend to occur more frequently in women during adolescence, pregnancy, the postpartum period (the first few months after giving birth), perimenopause (the time leading up to menopause), and menopause (a natural decline in reproductive hormones that usually occurs during a woman's forties or fifties). These are all times of significant hormonal change. During these times women who have never had anxiety may have panic attacks, which can develop into panic disorder. "There is absolutely a connection between hormonal changes and psychiatric symptoms in general, and women undergoing specific hormonal changes have increased risk for particular psychiatric disorders," says psychiatrist and anxiety expert Jason Schiffman. "With respect to anxiety, women in the perimenopausal period are more likely to experience panic attacks and other anxiety symptoms than other women of the same age who are either pre- or postmenopausal."[20]

In addition to hormonal changes, some people believe that women have an increased risk of developing panic disorders because they face increased cultural pressure to meet other's needs before their own, which causes stress. Others suggest that women are more likely to be diagnosed with a panic disorder because they are more willing to visit a doctor and self-report panic and anxiety symptoms.

> "Women in the perimenopausal period are more likely to experience panic attacks and other anxiety symptoms than other women of the same age who are either pre- or postmenopausal."[20]
>
> —Jason Schiffman, a psychiatrist and anxiety expert.

Heredity

There is also evidence that genes may be a factor in who develops panic disorder. A person with a close relative who suffers from panic disorder has an increased risk of developing it as well. According to the University of Maryland Medical Center, up to 50 percent of people with panic disorder have a close relative with the disorder.

Studies with twins have confirmed the possibility that panic disorder is inherited, according to the American Psychological Association. Several genes have been identified as possibly linked to panic disorder, and scientists believe that multiple genes act together to determine a person's vulnerability to anxiety and panic disorder. Still, it is unclear which genes are involved and how exactly they interact to heighten risk.

In 2011 a study published in the journal *Biological Psychiatry* identified cell material that might act as a molecular "switch" to control groups of genes implicated in panic disorder. Ribonucleic acid, or

The human brain makes it possible to feel fear, anxiety, and panic. For example, the amygdala and frontal cortex are involved in generating feelings of anxiety. Another part of the brain, called the periaquaductal grey, is involved in regulating a person's defensive or protective behaviors. Scientists hope that by better understanding the parts of the brain that are involved in producing and regulating the biological processes of fear and panic they will be able to develop more targeted and effective treatments for people with panic disorder.

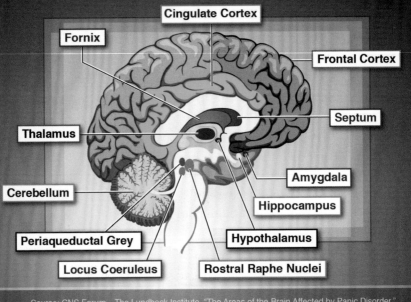

Source: CNS Forum—The Lundbeck Institute, "The Areas of the Brain Affected by Panic Disorder." www.cns.forum.com.

RNA, is created in the body's cells. Each cell's nucleus holds instructions for life, called deoxyribonucleic acid (DNA). RNA is used to copy the DNA instructions and take them to the necessary parts of the cell so it can carry out its function, such as making a particular protein. MicroRNAs (miRNAs) are small parts of RNA that bind to DNA and control the expression of different genes.

Researchers studying miRNA found that at least four types may be linked to panic disorder. Further studies have found that these miRNAs repress several genes that scientists suspect may be involved in the brain's regulation of anxiety. As John Krystal, editor of *Biological Psychiatry*, put it, "Variation in genes coding for miRNAs may coordinate the involvement of a number of risk genes and thereby contribute to the development of panic disorder."[21]

In 2013 researchers from the Centre for Genomic Regulation (CRG) in Spain announced that they had discovered a specific gene—NTRK3—that may be linked to panic disorder. NTRK3 is responsible for encoding a protein essential to brain formation, keeping neurons alive, and developing connections between neurons. In healthy people genes like NTRK3 are regulated, which means they are switched on and off so that they are expressed at the proper times. However, when NTRK3 is deregulated and the controls that turn it on and off are not in place, this gene appears to increase a person's perception of fear, which makes them likely to overestimate danger and have a heightened sense of alarm and anxiety.

"We have observed that deregulation of NTRK3 produces changes in brain development that lead to malfunctions in the fear-related memory system," explains Mara Dierssen, head of the Cellular and Systems Neurobiology group at the CRG. "In particular, this system is more efficient at processing information to do with fear

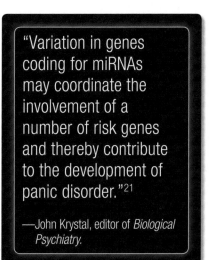

"Variation in genes coding for miRNAs may coordinate the involvement of a number of risk genes and thereby contribute to the development of panic disorder."[21]

—John Krystal, editor of *Biological Psychiatry.*

. . . and, also, [it] stores that information in a more lasting and consistent manner."[22] In other words, when NTRK3 is not regulated properly, it changes the brain's fear memory system. It makes this system both more sensitive to fear triggers and better able to store fear memories.

Although there has been some progress in understanding the genetic component of panic disorder, scientists believe much work remains in this area. At the same time, researchers believe that other factors, such as brain function and chemistry, environment, and stress, also play a role in the development of panic disorder.

Suffocation Alarm

Many people with panic disorder have shortness of breath and feel like they are going to suffocate. In the brain, humans have a suffocation alarm system, which alerts the body to the threat of suffocation and a decrease in available oxygen. This system originally developed to protect humans; it triggers a fight-or-flight stress response when the body senses the threat of suffocation. In people with panic disorder, however, this suffocation alarm system may be overly sensitive. For example, studies have shown that breathing air with increased carbon dioxide levels can trigger panic attacks in disordered people, whereas breathing the same air does not bother people without the disorder.

Researchers suspect that the overly sensitive suffocation alarm may be linked to a variation of a particular gene that regulates carbon dioxide anxiety. In 2014 a collaborative group of international researchers reported that different forms of the ACCN2 gene appeared to be associated with panic disorder. The gene variant's effect was stronger in people who reported respiratory symptoms such as shortness of breath and feelings of suffocation during panic attacks.

Panic Disorder and the Brain

Researchers know that several parts of the brain are involved in regulating fear and anxiety. Changes to these parts and in how they function may play a role in who develops panic disorder. Using sophisticated brain imaging technology such as magnetic resonance imaging (MRI) and functional magnetic resonance imaging, researchers can look at detailed images of the brain's structures and how it operates. Scientists have used these techniques to identify areas of the brain that are associated with fear responses, such as the limbic system.

The limbic system plays an important role in how a person experiences emotion, especially fear and reward emotions. It is made up of several structures, including the amygdalae, hippocampus, thalamus, hypothalamus, fornix, and cingulate gyrus. The parts of the limbic system have multiple connections with each other and with other parts of the brain.

Within the limbic system, the amygdalae are a pair of almond-shaped structures located deep in the brain and made up of clusters of neurons. When triggered by stimuli, the amygdalae regulate fear, memory, and emotion and coordinate the body's physical responses such as heart rate and blood pressure. A healthy person feels fear in response to an emotional or environmental trigger. This can be something seen or heard, like a mysterious shadow or a sudden noise. The trigger can also be something smelled, tasted, or felt. Even internal thoughts may act as a trigger in some cases.

The amygdalae react to the trigger by preparing the body to fight or run away. Triggers that are related to past emotional experiences produce a stronger reaction in the amygdalae, which are also involved in long-term memory storage. The amygdalae relay messages to other structures in the brain and body to release certain chemicals and hormones into the bloodstream that tell the body to fight or flee. One such structure is the adrenal glands, which release the chemical epinephrine (also known as adrenaline) into the bloodstream. Epinephrine makes the body's processes speed up; for example, it increases blood sugar for quick energy and increases heart rate. The body shakes to distribute the blood to the extremities, and the breathing rate increases so that there is enough oxygen for the increased blood flow.

Because the amygdalae are an important part of fear processing, scientists believe that irregular activity or structural changes in them may be linked to panic disorder. Specifically, scientists believe that panic attacks occur when there is abnormal activity in the amygdalae's cluster of nerves. In a 2012 review of existing research, scientists at Ewha Womans University in Seoul, South Korea, noted that several animal studies link stimulation of the amygdalae to behavior that is similar to human panic attacks. In addition, the researchers noted that several MRI studies showed that patients with panic disorder had smaller amygdalae than patients without the disorder, with greater reduction in the right amygdala than the left amygdala. The researchers concluded that "the amygdala, the hub of fear processing networks, is closely associated with the pathogenesis of PD [panic disorder] as well as panic attack."[23]

> "The amygdala, the hub of fear processing networks, is closely associated with the pathogenesis of PD [panic disorder] as well as panic attack."[23]
>
> —Researchers at Ewha Womans University in Seoul, South Korea.

People with panic disorder may have abnormalities in brain development that might affect the way memories of a panic attack are stored in the brain. In the 2013 CRG study, for example, the hippocampus of people with panic disorder was overactive. In a healthy person the hippocampus forms memories and processes contextual information. Abnormalities in the hippocampus, however, can cause a person to have exaggerated formation of fear memories, which may contribute to panic disorder.

Biochemistry

Studies suggest that brain chemistry may also play a role in panic disorder. Neurotransmitters are chemicals in the brain that send signals across gaps called synapses between the brain's nerve cells. Neurotransmitters affect how a person feels, thinks, and behaves. Research has shown that people with anxiety often have imbalances in certain neurotransmitters that can cause the brain's messages to be delivered incorrectly or not at all. Because panic disorder involves an overly sensitive fear response, researchers believe that imbalances in the neurotransmitters involved in the fear response are linked to this disorder. Neurotransmitters linked to panic disorder include serotonin, norepinephrine, epinephrine, dopamine, and gamma-aminobutyric acid (GABA).

When someone becomes anxious, the brain signals the body to release norepinephrine and epinephrine, which prepare a person for a fight-or-flight response. The release of epinephrine speeds up heart rate, increases respiratory rate, and triggers other physical changes. Norepinephrine also has a stimulating effect. It improves alertness and plays a role in long-term memory and learning. Optimal levels of norepinephrine during a stressful situation can give a person a sense of well-being, whereas excess levels of the neurotransmitter can increase physical symptoms of fear and anxiety. Serotonin, a different neurotransmitter, regulates feelings of well-being and mood. Low levels of serotonin have been linked to both anxiety and depression. Studies have shown that panic and anxiety can be improved by therapy and medications that increase the brain's serotonin levels.

Imbalances in the neurotransmitter GABA may be similarly linked to panic and anxiety. GABA acts as an inhibitory neu-

A young couple engages in a stressful conversation about money. In some instances, experts say, stressful life events can trigger panic even in people who have not experienced symptoms of panic disorder.

rotransmitter; it slows down activity of neurons in the central nervous system when it binds to a GABA receptor. It calms down and balances excited neurons. Some researchers believe that one of GABA's roles is to control the fear and anxiety individuals experience when their neurons are overstimulated. In panic disorder, attacks may be caused by interference with GABA receptor function, especially in the amygdalae, midbrain, and hypothalamus. Studies suggest that if GABA levels are low, a person may exhibit signs of stress and anxiety.

Bullying Increases Risk of Future Panic Disorder

Bullying can take many forms, including verbal, emotional, physical, and cyber. It can happen at school, work, or even at home. According to a 2013 study partially funded by the NIMH, the effect of bullying can linger long into adulthood, putting bullies and victims at higher risk for mental illnesses such as anxiety and depression when they become adults.

In the study, researchers from Duke University interviewed a sample of 1,420 children over several years and followed them into adulthood. The researchers found that those children who reported being bullied had four times the risk of developing agoraphobia, generalized anxiety, and panic disorder as adults than those children who reported being neither a bully nor a victim. Those who identified as bully-victims—who both bullied others and were bullied themselves—were at an even higher risk. Bully-victims were fourteen times more likely to develop panic disorder, five times more likely to develop depressive disorders, and ten times more likely to have suicidal thoughts. Researchers say their results suggest that efforts to reduce bullying could also reduce incidence of panic disorder and other mental illnesses.

Because neurotransmitters often work together and rely on each other for function, an imbalance in one may affect others. For example, GABA only functions properly when there are adequate amounts of serotonin in the brain. Panic disorder, along with several other mental illnesses, may therefore be caused by the ripple effect of too much or too little of certain neurotransmitters.

Hormones

Scientists are also studying how hormones affect panic disorder. Hormones are chemicals that help the body's organs function. Hormones help a person grow and develop correctly; they also play a role in regulating metabolism. Imbalances in certain hormones, however, can be a factor in panic attacks, causing a fight-or-flight response to be triggered when there is no real threat or danger.

Excess levels of certain hormones have been linked to panic attacks. For example, the stress hormones cortisol and epinephrine (also a neurotransmitter) are released when the body experiences stress. They activate the body's fight-or-flight response when facing a stressful or threatening situation. In addition, the excess production of thyroid hormone, a medical condition known as hyperthyroidism, has been linked to a stress response like that experienced in a panic attack, including increased heart rate, increased breathing, and excessive sweating.

Brain pH and Acidity

Other research suggests that increased acidity or low pH in the brain may be linked to panic disorders. In one 2009 study, researchers at the University of Iowa showed that carbon dioxide increased brain acidity in mice, which in turn activated a brain protein that has an essential role in panic and anxiety behavior.

The researchers tested the mice's brain acidity when they breathed in carbon dioxide. They found that the inhaled carbon dioxide raised brain acidity, which in turn activated the ASIc1a protein in the amygdala. This increased fear behavior in the mice. The mice's fear memory was also enhanced when the carbon dioxide activated the protein. "This is a new finding that the amygdala, which is considered the brain's computer processor for fear, can also function as a sensor for detecting chemical signals—carbon dioxide and acidity (low pH)— that are known to trigger panic attacks in susceptible individuals,"[24] says lead researcher John Wemmie.

In another study, the same team of University of Iowa researchers tested the effects of brain acidity on human volunteers. They used a blinking checkerboard to stimulate the area of the brain that interprets visual sensory input. As the participants viewed the checkerboard's flashes, an MRI recorded changes in brain pH. The scientists noted that a decrease in pH, which signals a rise in brain acidity, occurred when the region became more active. They suspect that these changes in pH due to brain activity may affect pH-sensitive receptors in the brain. This in turn may activate proteins that enhance the fear response and may play a role in triggering panic attacks.

Environmental Factors

In addition to genetic and biological factors, researchers are also studying the role of stress and other environmental factors in panic disorder. Everyone experiences stress at some point. Stress can come from relationships, work, school, and finances. Stress is common when a loved one dies or a job is lost. Even positive events such as the birth of a child or moving in to a new house can cause stress. Stress is a normal part of life, yet everyone handles it differently.

In some cases stress is a trigger for the onset of panic and other anxiety disorders. If a person has a genetic or biological vulnerability to panic and anxiety, a stressful event may be the environmental factor that triggers the disorder, turning it on like a light switch. According to the American Psychiatric Association, a major stressful life event—such as a birth, divorce, accident, or death—can trigger a panic attack in a person who has never before had an attack nor displayed any symptoms of panic disorder. There is a sensitive interaction between genetic, biological, and environmental factors, which may explain why one person develops panic disorder while another who experiences the same stressful event does not.

Many people who suffer from panic disorder cannot point to a specific stressful event that triggered its onset. For these people, the cumulative effect of chronic stress may be a factor in their illness. In 2011 researchers from Brown University studied how daily stress such as fighting with a partner or pressures at work can affect the symptoms of panic. They found that some types of stressful events cause panic symptoms to increase gradually over time, rather than trigger an immediate panic reaction. "We definitely expected the symptoms to get worse over time, but we also thought the symptoms would get worse right away,"[25] says Ethan Moitra of the Warren Alpert Medical School at Brown University.

In their study, researchers reviewed annual assessments of 418 adults with panic disorder over a six-year period. The assessments asked participants detailed questions about important events in their lives and their corresponding anxiety levels. After a statistical analysis of the results, researchers found that stressful life events relating to two categories—"work" and "friends/family/household"—caused panic symptoms to increase steadily but gradually for at least twelve weeks after the initial event. In other categories such as "crime/legal," stressful events did not appear to affect the participant's panic symptoms. The researchers say that this gradual increase in panic weeks after stressful life events may be one reason why many people cannot pinpoint a single event that prompted feelings of panic. "This may be one of those reasons why panic disorders can get worse,"[26] Moitra said.

When stress continues over a period of months or years, it accumulates. This stress is more enduring than the normal, temporary stress of, say, moving to a new town or starting a new job. Cumulative stress may exist because of long-standing difficulties in a person's life, such as problems in a marriage or a difficult relationship with a parent. It may also be the accumulation of many life events, such as changing jobs, moving to a new city, having children, and so on. Most people experience a major life event from time to time, but having a series of several major events over a short period can cause stress to build up in a way that leads to chronic panic.

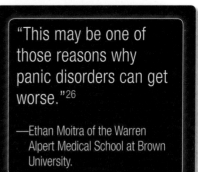

"This may be one of those reasons why panic disorders can get worse."[26]

—Ethan Moitra of the Warren Alpert Medical School at Brown University.

Medical Factors, Substance Use, and Nutritional Deficiencies

In some cases a medical condition can cause panic attacks. Certain conditions disrupt brain chemistry and function, causing an inappropriate fear response. Hyperthyroidism and hypoglycemia (low blood sugar) can cause panic attacks that appear identical to those experienced in panic disorder. Some heart conditions, such as mitral valve prolapse, which occurs when one of the heart's valves does not close properly, can also cause panic attacks. When these medical conditions are corrected, the panic symptoms go away.

Nutritional deficiencies have also been linked to panic disorder. The human body needs vitamins and other nutrients for neurotransmitters and hormonal systems to function properly; malfunctions in these systems are tied to panic disorder. Vitamin C and magnesium are two nutrients that are key components in stress regulation. When a person goes through a stressful period, his or her body uses and excretes greater amounts of vitamin C and magnesium than during low-stress periods. The body uses magnesium to prevent excitatory

Panic attacks have a variety of causes. One cause might be a condition in which the valves of the heart (pictured) do not close properly.

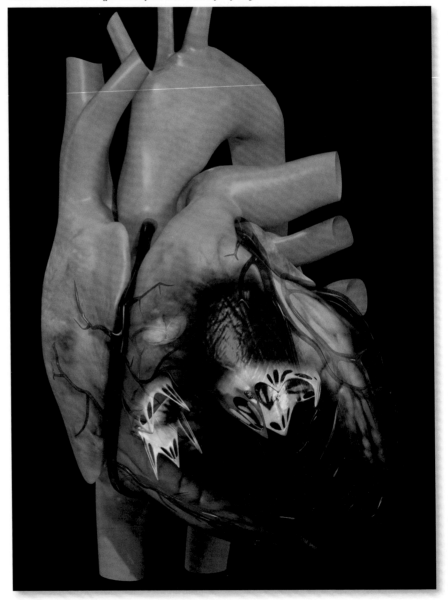

neurotransmitters (which stimulate the brain) from overfiring, and this helps reduce stress. Meanwhile, the adrenal glands hold high concentrations of vitamin C and can shrink when vitamin C levels decrease. This in turn makes them less able to make the hormones the body needs to properly respond to stress and can lead to a slower recovery from panic and anxiety. Other nutrients linked to anxiety and panic disorder include vitamin B, calcium, and iron. If a person does not have enough of these nutrients, he or she may be less able to deal with stress, which can lead to anxiety, panic attacks, and eventually panic disorder.

Many Factors

It is unclear why some people are able to deal with stress and fear but others develop a full-blown disorder. Most scientists believe that there is no single cause of panic disorder but rather that it develops from a combination of many factors. Through research, scientists hope to better identify and understand the factors that influence a person's vulnerability to panic.

CHAPTER 3

What Is It like to Live with Panic Disorder?

Panic disorder can be very frightening and debilitating, and it can seriously affect a person's quality of life. This disorder can have a devastating emotional and social impact, damaging relationships with family and friends and impairing a person's ability to work and go to school. People with panic disorder often spend less time on hobbies, sports, and other pleasurable activities. Because panic attacks can disrupt their ability to hold a job, sufferers are more likely to be financially dependent on others. Having a panic disorder can also increase a person's risk of developing other mental health disorders such as depression. People who struggle with panic disorder are also more likely to develop substance abuse problems and have suicidal thoughts.

One person who lives like this is Ms. K, a twenty-four-year-old waitress who began to experience unpredictable panic attacks. Occurring multiple times per week, the attacks forced Ms. K to leave work and cancel shifts. Since the attacks began, Ms. K says that she has become preoccupied with the idea that she is going to die from a catastrophic illness. Instead of enjoying hobbies and activities with friends, she spends her time researching symptoms on the Internet. Her panic attacks have sent her to the emergency room, where doctors could find no physical cause for her symptoms. Unable to control her attacks, Ms. K says that panic has made her life feel extremely limited. She believes that her future dreams of going to nursing school and starting a family seem out of reach.

Like Ms. K, many panic disorder sufferers find that every single aspect of their life—from work, to school, to relationships, to socializing, to running simple errands and even taking a shower—is significantly affected by their disorder. "Once, a friend asked me to explain what things I couldn't do," says sufferer Neal Sideman. "I answered that it would take much less time if I simply listed those things I could do."[27]

Living with the Physical Effects

Although panic disorder is a mental illness, it also affects people physically. Panic affects each person differently. Some people experience increased heart rate, sweating, headaches, trembling, chest pain, and shortness of breath. They may get chills or experience hot flashes. They may have nausea and abdominal cramping. Others feel dizzy and faint or a tingling in their hands or feet. Their throats tighten and they have trouble swallowing. "I was a 15-year-old waitress going about my business when I felt a strange, flickering sensation in the center of my chest," remembers Priscilla Warner, a best-selling author who suffers from panic disorder. "My lungs tightened, my throat closed up, my head started spinning and my heart began to pound. I was having a panic attack."[28]

The physical effects of panic disorder can become so disruptive that they drive a person to a doctor. If the doctor cannot find a physical cause of the problem, he or she may suggest the patient undergo a psychological evaluation to determine if the patient is suffering from panic disorder or another mental illness.

> "I felt a strange, flickering sensation in the center of my chest. My lungs tightened, my throat closed up, my head started spinning and my heart began to pound. I was having a panic attack."[28]
>
> —Priscilla Warner, a best-selling author who suffers from panic disorder.

Over time this level of chronic stress and anxiety can leave its mark on the body. Excess stress hormones that are released during the fight-or-flight response constrict blood vessels and elevate a person's blood pressure. Anxiety and stress also affect the immune system, decreasing the number of white blood cells, which fight bacteria and viruses. This puts a person at a higher risk of developing certain infections and illnesses.

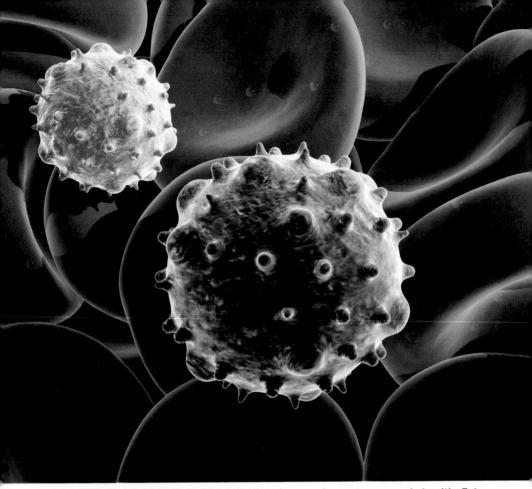

The anxiety of living with panic disorder can damage a person's health. Extreme stress can lead to a decrease in the body's disease-fighting white blood cells (pictured), which in turn can make a person vulnerable to infection and illness.

For example, panic disorder has been linked to an increased risk of heart disease. A 2008 study from researchers with the European Society of Cardiology found that people who suffer from panic attacks or panic disorder had a significantly higher risk of developing heart disease or having a heart attack than people without the disorder, particularly if they were under fifty years old when first diagnosed.

The researchers reviewed the primary care medical records for 57,615 adults diagnosed with panic attacks or disorder and 347,039 adults without the disorder. They found that adults age fifty or younger with panic disorder were at least 38 percent more likely to have a heart attack and 44 percent more likely to develop heart disease than adults without the disorder. "Not much is known about the relationship between panic disorder and cardiac disease," says Dr. Kate Walters, a senior lecturer in primary care at University College London, who led the research. "The symptoms of panic attacks can closely mimic those of a heart attack or acute cardiac disease, and it seems that there may be a complex relationship between them."[29]

Although researchers state that the link between panic disorder and increased risk of heart disease is not completely understood, they speculate that this linkage may be due to several factors. In some cases doctors may initially misdiagnose coronary heart disease as panic attacks. In other cases there may be a true increase in coronary heart disease and heart attack in patients caused by panic disorder. Repeated activation of the sympathetic nervous system during panic attacks can clog arteries and alter normal heart rates, both of which are risk factors for heart disease.

Emotional and Social Impacts

Living with panic disorder can deeply impact a person's emotional state. Constant worrying and feeling uncontrollable fear can make individuals feel scared, unprotected, and constantly on guard. Chronic worrying and stress can cause them to become overwhelmed by everyday situations. As a result, they may have trouble concentrating and become irritable and restless. Many people with panic disorder are embarrassed of their illness and try to hide their symptoms from others. They may fear being unfairly judged by others as weak. As a result, many people struggling with panic feel misunderstood or alone.

Relationships with partners, family, and friends suffer when panic disorder sufferers adapt their behavior to avoid places and situations they fear may trigger an attack. They may make excuses to avoid going to public places or taking public transportation. They may stop attending social events. When they do go out, some insist on sitting near doors or exits so they can leave in a hurry. Over time these changes cause them to spend less time on hobbies, sports, and other activities that they previously enjoyed.

The experience of a woman named Kelly is illustrative of how panic disorder can, over time, isolate a person from the rest of the world. Kelly had her first panic attack while driving, and it was so awful that thereafter she had trouble getting into a car and stopped driving on highways entirely. This behavior continued as each place she had a panic attack became off-limits or avoided. She explains:

> I had them at movie theaters or concerts—so I stopped going to those places. I stopped going to the mall, to the grocery store, or flying. I stopped going anywhere alone with my children because I was afraid of what might happen to them if I fainted or died while we were out. Eventually, I stopped going anywhere alone. I quit my job and sold my car and relied on my husband to take me and the children everywhere. I remember every day seeming gray and cloudy, and every day I cried.[30]

Relationships Strained

In many cases these drastic behavior changes can seriously strain relationships. Marriages are among the first relationships to suffer. This was the case with Kara Baskin, the Boston editor of *New York* magazine's food blog *Grub Street*. When she got married, her panic disorder nearly ruined her Maui honeymoon.

> I actually spent my vacation in sweat pants, eating room-service burritos from a Styrofoam tray while propped on pillows, stuffing myself like some deranged queen, watching 'The Golden Girls' reruns while my husband paced from my bedside to the balcony that overlooked a golf course. . . . Every morning, he'd unlock the hotel-room safe, look at our plane tickets and wander outside."[31]

Baskin says that years of panic attacks peaked on her honeymoon, resulting in agoraphobia. Although she made it through her wedding, she suffered a wave of severe panic attacks on the trip. She explains:

> At dinner, I shivered in the hot breeze, convinced that there was poison in my sushi. I returned to the hotel and riffled through our welcome packet, flipping to the Emergency Services section to confirm there was a resort doctor on duty. I mapped routes to hospitals. I left our room approximately five

Caffeine and Anxiety

Caffeine is a stimulant commonly found in coffee, tea, chocolate, cocoa, sodas, and energy drinks. When consumed, caffeine gives a boost of energy and increases mental alertness and focus. However, some people with panic disorder and other anxiety disorders find that they are more sensitive than others to the effects of caffeine. Caffeine can cause subtle physical changes such as increased heart rate, upset stomach, or increased mental focus. Many people who suffer from panic disorder are hypersensitive to these changes and fear they may signal the start of a panic attack. As a result, ingesting caffeine actually ends up triggering a panic attack in some people. For these reasons, many doctors recommend that panic disorder patients reduce or eliminate caffeine from their diet.

times. Our longest outing was a luau, which I endured by guzzling four cocktails in an hour.[32]

Parents of sufferers also have a hard time coping when their child has panic disorder. Katherine C. Cowan, whose daughter Sara has panic disorder, knows these difficulties firsthand. She says:

> Parents can be significantly affected by their children's mental health problems and often need support themselves. You would do anything to take your child's pain from them, including absorbing it yourself. I frequently teetered on the brink of Sara's suffering, dealing with my own stress and anxiety while trying to balance work and the rest of the family's needs. This can be very isolating, particularly for families afraid of stigma.[33]

Problems with Work and School

Panic and anxiety can also cause problems at work and school. Symptoms can make it difficult to concentrate and meet deadlines. Individuals may turn down a promotion or opportunity because it involves panic-inducing travel or public speaking. Afraid of having a panic attack in public, they might make excuses to avoid office parties, staff lunches, meetings with coworkers, and school events. For people with agoraphobia, simply leaving their house to get to work or school can be difficult.

Anna Williamson, a business reporter for the British television show *Daybreak*, says that panic attacks almost ruined her career. She suffered her first panic attack in 2007, and the attacks began to occur more frequently until she was suffering attacks every day. "The worst attacks happened when I was about to start filming," she says. "I spent a lot of time hiding in the bathroom saying, 'Come on, you can do this.'" Her breaking point came when she showed up at work without sleeping at all the night before. When a coworker asked her if she was all right, she burst into tears. "I was ushered out of the building, put in a taxi and told to get whatever help I needed,"[34] she says. Williamson saw her doctor, who prescribed antianxiety medication, and also started seeing a psychiatrist.

"I spent a lot of time hiding in the bathroom saying, 'Come on, you can do this.'"[34]

—Anna Williamson, a business reporter who experienced panic attacks at work.

Substance Abuse

People who have panic disorder may turn to alcohol or drugs to calm themselves. Alcohol and other drugs affect receptors in the brain in a way that reduces stress, though only temporarily. Although this may provide short-term relief, in the long term alcohol and other substances can actually make panic symptoms worse and can even trigger attacks.

Indeed, drinking or doing drugs can worsen other problems in people's lives, which in turn typically causes them more anxiety and panic. In this way abusing substances can become a vicious cycle: The individuals drink or take drugs to relieve anxiety, which leads to more problems, panic, and anxiety. By the time the person realizes that alcohol or drugs are not helping them deal with their panic attacks, they may feel as if they cannot stop using these substances.

People with panic disorder sometimes turn to alcohol or drugs for relief. But the kind of relief these substances provide lasts only a short time.

Frequent alcohol and drug use can result in a substance abuse problem and can even trigger attacks. ABC News anchor Dan Harris is one person who knows this firsthand. In 2004 Harris had an attack on live television. "Shortly after seven on a sunny spring morning in 2004, I freaked out in front of five million people," writes Harris, who was filling in on the news show *Good Morning America*. He describes the experience in the following way:

I was overtaken by a massive, irresistible blast of fear. It felt like the world was ending. My heart was thumping. I was gasping for air. I had pretty much lost the ability to speak. And all of it was compounded by the knowledge that my freak-out was being broadcast live on national television. Halfway through the six stories I was supposed to read, I simply bailed, squeaking out a "Back to you."[35]

In a 2014 blog entry, Harris revealed that his panic attacks were likely caused by drug use. More than a decade earlier, he had been in the field covering the wars in Afghanistan and Iraq, as well as conflict between Israel and the Palestinian territories. The violence and sadness he encountered left him feeling anxious, depressed, and off-kilter, almost bored. Once back in the United States, he began to self-medicate with drugs such as cocaine and ecstasy. In hindsight, Harris thinks he took these drugs to re-create the thrill of the war zone. According to his doctor, however, the drugs actually increased the level of adrenaline in his brain, making him more vulnerable to panic attacks. Harris's doctor explained to him that such substances left a lasting impact on his brain chemistry and increased his risk of panic.

How to Help During a Panic Attack

If a person has a panic attack, there are several things friends and family can do to help the person get through it. The person in the middle of an attack may become very anxious and have trouble thinking clearly. Friends and family should remain calm and stay with the person. Other tips include moving to a quiet place, offering medicine if the person usually takes it during an attack, and asking if the person needs water, more or less light, or other help altering the environment.

Friends and family can help the person focus by speaking in short, simple sentences and asking the sufferer to repeat a simple, physical task, such as raising the person's arms over his or her head to distract the person from thoughts of fear. Friends and family may want to reassure the person that he or she will get through the attack and remind the person that although he or she may be scared, there is no actual danger. Breathing with the person or counting slowly can help slow breathing. By offering calming support during an attack, friends and family may be able to prevent the attack from getting worse.

Harris is not alone. According to the ADAA, people with panic and other anxiety disorders are two to three times more likely to have an alcohol or other substance abuse disorder in their lifetime than people without these disorders. According to Mental Health America, 30 percent of people with panic disorder use alcohol, and approximately 17 percent abuse illegal drugs such as cocaine and marijuana in an attempt to relieve stress.

Suicide

For some people the stress of living with panic disorder can lead to suicidal thoughts and attempts to take their own life. According to Mental Health America, approximately 20 percent of people with panic disorder attempt suicide. Individuals with panic disorder and a mood disorder such as depression have an even higher risk of suicide.

For example, consider the tragic case of Josh Marks. In 2012 Marks, a rising chef, had beaten out thousands of contestants to finish in second place on Gordon Ramsay's competition television show *MasterChef*. After the show's taping in 2012, Marks began to have debilitating panic attacks. According to this family, he was eventually diagnosed with bipolar disorder and schizophrenia, along with the panic attacks. Unable to deal with his illnesses, in 2013 Marks ended his life by shooting himself.

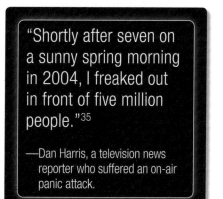

"Shortly after seven on a sunny spring morning in 2004, I freaked out in front of five million people."[35]

—Dan Harris, a television news reporter who suffered an on-air panic attack.

Zimri Yaseen, a psychiatrist with the Department of Psychiatry and Behavioral Sciences at Beth Israel Medical Center, reports that there is a link between panic and suicide, though researchers are still trying to figure out exactly what it might be. "We need to better understand the acute state that might trigger suicide," says Yaseen. "We think that in many cases the acute state might be a panic-like state."[36] Igor Galynker, a psychiatrist at Beth Israel Medical Center, agrees, explaining that when people feel trapped and like they have no options, they start to panic; this distorts their cognition and impairs judgment, which makes them more prone to commit suicide.

In a 2012 study, Yaseen, Galynker, and colleagues further investigated the link between panic and suicide. They examined data from 2,864 patients and determined that those who had panic attacks in the previous year were more likely to think about and attempt suicide. Simply having a panic attack, however, was not enough to trigger an increased risk of suicide. The study found that patients who were afraid of dying during a panic attack had seven times the risk of attempting suicide. The researchers hope their findings will help doctors better treat and prevent suicide in patients with panic attacks and panic disorder. "We think it is important for clinicians to ask about panic attacks and pay particular attention to what panic symptoms the patient has," says Yaseen, "because those symptoms can be a significant warning sign that trouble is brewing."[37]

According to the American Foundation for Suicide Prevention, most suicides are preventable. Even so, many people with mental illnesses such as panic disorder never seek help from qualified mental health professionals. Often those who are most at risk for suicide fail to receive treatment because of the stigma of mental illness, lack of access to care, or a lack of knowledge about their disorder and its symptoms. Better access to information and treatment could therefore significantly improve outcomes for those who struggle with panic disorder.

Supporting a Loved One with Panic Disorder

Panic disorders affect a wide circle of people beyond the person diagnosed. Family, friends, and coworkers are among the many people who are impacted when someone in their lives is coping with a panic disorder. Supporting a person who suffers from a panic disorder can be difficult, and partners, family, and friends often struggle with how best to help.

Experts such as Todd Farchione, a clinical psychologist at Boston University, recommend offering gentle encouragement when a person is having a panic attack. "If you really want to help somebody, then the way you should go about it is to ask yourself if you can be supportive of

Supportive family and friends can help a person who has panic disorder. Providing that support, however, can be difficult at times.

the individual in a way that allows them to tell you about what they're experiencing and why they may be experiencing that,"[38] he says. Telling a person having an attack that there is nothing to worry about can actually increase the person's panic, so Farchione recommends avoiding that. He also stresses that it is important to remain calm during the attack. Even though a panic attack can be frightening to witness, it will pass. Adding more panic and emotion to the situation is usually unhelpful. Allison Baker, a child and adolescent psychiatrist, recommends that since sufferers know their anxiety and panic better than anyone, witnesses should take cues from them. "Take your direction from the person themselves instead of going on the assumption of what they may need from you,"[39] says Baker. Because panic attacks feel different for each person, the individual will usually know what he or she needs—whether it is a shoulder to cry on, a glass of water, or a breath of fresh air.

At the same time, experts such as Baker and Farchione warn family and friends to avoid enabling the person's panic attacks. There is a difference between being understanding and being accommodating. By accommodating fears, family members may just end up reinforcing the person's belief that there really is something to fear.

Living with Panic Disorder

Panic disorder sufferers must learn to live with the many physical, emotional, and social effects of their illness. In spite of these challenges, many are able to live normal and productive lives. One such inspiration is Stacy Gregg, who experienced her first panic attack in sixth grade. She suffered repeated attacks, and by college her disorder had become so threatening that an urgent care doctor recommended she drop out of school.

Instead, Gregg decided to take back her life. "I learned to control my panic attacks through therapy, self-help books, and my amazing best friend, Stephanie, who has always been there for me and never passes judgment," says Gregg. After several years of work, Gregg finished college and even obtained a graduate degree in business. "Although I still worry and get anxious, I haven't let my anxiety disorders control my life: Now I control them."[40]

CHAPTER 4

Can Panic Disorder Be Treated or Cured?

Those who struggle with panic disorder may feel like nothing can help them escape the never-ending cycle of attacks. Panic disorder is treatable, however. In fact, treatment can bring significant relief for the majority of people who suffer from panic disorder. In addition, receiving treatment early can stop the disorder from progressing to a more severe form and also prevent the onset of agoraphobia.

Panic disorder is typically treated with psychotherapy, medication, or a combination of the two. Because every patient responds differently to treatment, a successful plan considers a person's specific needs. With appropriate treatment, most patients see an improvement within a few weeks or months, and very likely within a year, according to the American Psychological Association.

Diagnosis

The first step in treating panic disorder is to get an accurate diagnosis. Panic attacks often cause symptoms that are similar to physical conditions that involve the heart and lungs, such as heart attacks and chest pain. Many people who are eventually diagnosed with panic disorder first seek medical help because they think they have a life-threatening medical condition.

To begin, a doctor will carefully evaluate a patient to determine whether his or her symptoms stem from a physical problem. The doctor may perform a physical exam, order blood or urine tests, and ask detailed questions about a patient's symptoms and medical history. Certain conditions such as having excess thyroid hormones or cardiac arrhythmias—a disturbance in the heartbeat's rhythm—can cause symptoms that mimic a panic attack. These medical conditions must be ruled out before proceeding to a diagnosis of panic disorder.

If no physical cause can be found, the doctor or trained mental health professional may use a psychological questionnaire or otherwise interview the patient about symptoms, as well as take his or her family and personal history with mental illness. Questions usually involve whether the patient has experienced a recent traumatic event, if he or she drinks alcohol or uses drugs, and if certain situations or places trigger panic attacks.

If the patient is diagnosed with panic disorder, he or she will receive a treatment plan. Most people with panic disorder can be effectively treated with a combination of psychotherapy and medication. Certain lifestyle changes such as getting adequate exercise, sleep, and nutrition can also help reduce anxiety and the frequency of panic attacks. Treatment works differently for everyone, so patients may need to try different types of treatments and medications until they find a combination that works the best for them.

Sara Cowan struggled with fear and anxiety through most of her childhood. She was diagnosed with separation anxiety as a child and with depression and panic disorder as a teen. Although doctors put her on medication for depression, it did not improve her symptoms. "We switched medications and doctors a few times before getting the correct diagnosis," says her mother, Katherine, who is also the director of communications for the National Association of School Psychologists. "With ongoing therapy and medication, Sara learned to better manage her symptoms and respond more effectively when high stress triggered panic attacks,"[41] Katherine says.

Cognitive Behavioral Therapy

Cognitive behavioral therapy (CBT) is one of the most common treatments for panic disorders. CBT is a form of talk therapy, or psychotherapy, in which the patient talks to a trained mental health professional about what triggers their attacks and how they can learn to manage them. CBT can take place in individual, group, or family sessions and is typically customized to a patient's specific needs.

Recovery and Relapse

Although treatment helps many patients overcome panic disorder, studies suggest that many will also relapse, or experience symptoms again, at some point. According to a 2013 study, approximately 61 percent of women and 58 percent of men with panic disorder achieved recovery (that is, going two months with minimal or no symptoms), within two years of beginning treatment. After several years, however, many patients experience a relapse (that is, a full return of symptoms for a two-week period). Eight years after treatment, men had a recovery rate of 69 percent and a relapse rate of 21 percent, while women had a recovery rate of 76 percent but a relapse rate of 64 percent. These findings suggest that for many, panic disorder is a chronic condition.

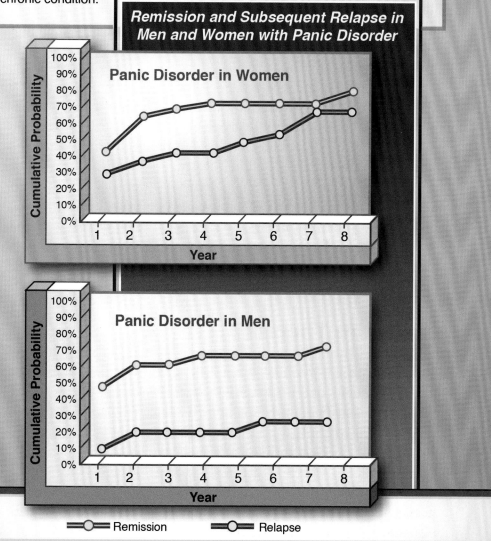

Remission and Subsequent Relapse in Men and Women with Panic Disorder

Source: Mark Vanelli, "Improving Treatment Response in Panic Disorder," *Primary Psychiatry*, May 21, 2013. http://primarypsychiatry.com.

CBT is based on the idea that people's thoughts influence their feelings and behaviors. During CBT therapists help patients change their perspective about their disorder. Because many sufferers worry they are going crazy or dying during an attack, CBT helps them recognize that their panic is based on a threat that is not real. Therapists also work with patients to develop skills and techniques to react appropriately to anxiety-producing situations. CBT can help patients identify possible triggers for attacks. A trigger can be a thought, a situation, or even a small change in heartbeat. Once patients learn to separate triggers from attacks, the triggers become less likely to induce future attacks. Therapists may also teach patients breathing exercises and other techniques to help them relax and relieve anxiety. In many cases, as patients work through their fears, they may experience temporary discomfort or increased feelings of anxiety.

Initial treatment with CBT generally occurs over a twelve-week period, and many sufferers find it effective. "My salvation—and that's what it genuinely felt like—came in the form of a short course of Cognitive Behavioral Therapy," says patient Lee Kynaston. "Short, intensely focused and ferociously logical, CBT is full of cool diagrams and homework and, as therapy goes, is exceptionally man-friendly." Kynaston says CBT helped him expose his irrational thoughts as exactly that—irrational and unnecessary. "Once you get this, and realize you're not going to die, you learn how to interrupt the cycle of anxiety, panic and fear,"[42] he says.

Exposure Therapy

A form of CBT called exposure therapy is a specific technique used to reduce patients' fear and anxiety responses over time. In exposure therapy, patients are literally asked to face their fears by being gradually and repeatedly exposed to their feared object, place, or situation. The exposure may initially occur through pictures or videos. Later the exposure takes place during real-life encounters. Often a therapist will go with a patient to the feared situation for support and guidance. As the exposure is repeated over time, the patient's anxious and fearful reactions decrease. Eventually, the patient learns to face the feared situation without feeling panic.

CART Breathing

In the middle of a panic attack, many people begin to hyperventilate. Hyperventilation is rapid or deep breathing and is also called overbreathing. It can leave a person feeling out of breath and worsens panic attack symptoms. When people hyperventilate, they exhale carbon dioxide too fast. Low carbon dioxide levels in the body cause the blood vessels to narrow, which restricts blood supply to the brain. As a result, the individuals feel light-headed and tingly. They may feel as if they are suffocating, when in reality they actually have too much air.

Based on this theory, researchers at Southern Methodist University developed a breathing therapy called capnometry-assisted respiratory therapy (CART) for panic attack sufferers to employ. Using CART, patients are taught to breathe slower and shallower by matching their breathing rate to a series of recorded tones. The patients use a machine called a capnometer to monitor their carbon dioxide and oxygen levels. The goal of the therapy is to reduce hyperventilation and related physical symptoms by breathing in a slow and shallow manner. The researchers hope that CART will help reduce panic in patients.

In treating panic disorder, exposure therapy tends to focus on exposing the patient to the physical sensations experienced during an attack. This is called interoceptive exposure. It is based on the fact that the root fear in panic disorder is the fear of another attack. Patients avoid situations and places not because they fear the place, but because they fear having an attack *at* that place. For example, individuals may avoid driving in cars not because they are afraid of vehicles, but because they fear being stuck in the car with no escape if a panic attack strikes.

Therapists may therefore help patients safely experience the symptoms of a panic attack in a controlled setting. To simulate the elevated heart rate, sweating, increased breathing, and dizziness that characterize a panic attack, patients will intentionally hyperventilate, run up and down stairs, or spin in a chair. Patients take note of what the symptoms feel like and then allow the symptoms to remain without trying to control them. Repeated exposure can help patients learn to temper their reaction to these symptoms so that the symptoms do not escalate into a full-blown attack. Interoceptive exposure usually begins with sessions in a safe environmen, such as a therapist's office, before progressing to other environments where patients can apply the techniques.

Exposure therapy may also be used to treat situational avoidance behaviors. Patients with agoraphobia can be gradually exposed to public situations. For example, they may take short trips away from home and slowly increase the duration and distance of the trips. Exposure therapy for agoraphobia often involves a patient's close friends or family, who offer support during sessions.

Although exposure therapy is generally a safe and effective treatment, some patients may find that it produces more anxiety and fear than they can handle. When this occurs, the patient is at risk of dropping out of treatment. In order to prevent dropout, the therapist should work with the patient to ensure that the anxiety produced during exposure treatments is not overwhelming, though still challenging enough to be effective. "Have an uncomfortable day," says psychologist Eric Goodman, who practices exposure therapy with patients at his Coastal Center for Anxiety Treatment. "It might be the key to a more comfortable future."[43]

Medication

In addition to therapy, a doctor may prescribe medication to help individuals control their panic attacks. Medication can be a short-term or long-term treatment, depending on the severity of a patient's symptoms and other individual considerations. The most common medications used to treat panic disorder are antidepressants, anti-anxiety drugs, and beta blockers.

Initially developed to treat depression, antidepressants are effective for many anxiety disorders, including panic disorder. Antidepressants work by adjusting brain chemicals such as serotonin to normal levels. Serotonin regulates feelings of well-being, and some studies suggest that decreased serotonin levels can lead to anxiety, panic, and depression. Although these medications begin to affect brain chemistry immediately, it usually takes about four to six weeks for patients to feel their full effect. Antidepressants include selective serotonin reuptake inhibitors (SSRIs), tricyclics, and monoamine oxidase inhibitors. SSRIs are particularly effective for reducing the symptoms of panic attacks, along with the anxiety, worry, and behavioral problems associated with panic disorder. Although most antidepressants are well tolerated by patients, some patients experience side effects such as nausea, nervousness, manic behavior, sexual dysfunction, headaches, dizziness, and weight gain while taking these medications.

Other medications frequently prescribed to panic disorder sufferers include benzodiazepines such as Xanax and Valium (diazepam). These drugs quickly relieve panic attack symptoms, relaxing a patient and reducing his or her symptoms almost immediately. Most benzodiazepines work to increase the amount or action of the GABA neurotransmitter in the brain. Because a patient can develop a tolerance to the medication and require increasingly higher doses in order to achieve the same effect, this type of medication is generally only used for a short time.

Singer Ellie Goulding is one person who has benefited from the use of benzodiazepines; her medication helped her control what had become debilitating panic attacks. "With the help of things like Diazepam in small doses to relax me at certain times, the attacks slowly stopped and now I'm through it,"[44] she says. Although effective, this medication's side effects include daytime drowsiness, lethargy, decreased reaction times, and trouble concentrating. Patients may also experience memory loss, dizziness, nausea, and loss of coordination.

Beta blockers are another medication used to treat panic disorder. Though they are generally used to treat heart conditions, they are sometimes prescribed to alleviate panic disorder's physical symptoms. Beta blockers target the receptors in the heart muscles, arteries, kidneys, and other organs associated with the sympathetic nervous

> "Have an uncomfortable day. It might be the key to a more comfortable future."[43]
>
> —Eric Goodman, a psychologist who practices exposure therapy with his patients.

system, which activates the body's fight-or-flight response. They interfere with the neurotransmitter epinephrine and certain stress hormones, which decreases the activation of the sympathetic nervous system. Beta blockers can inhibit symptoms of panic attacks such as sweating and increased heart rate. When a patient knows he or she will be in a situation that may cause an attack—such as flying or giv-

Medication has helped British singer Ellie Goulding (pictured) control her debilitating panic attacks. Benzodiazepines, which Goulding has taken, relax a person and almost immediately reduce panic symptoms.

ing a speech—a doctor can prescribe a beta blocker to temper panic's physical symptoms. Beta blockers are generally only used for a short time to treat panic disorder.

In some cases patients may decide to stop taking their medication without a doctor's approval. Some stop because they feel better and think they no longer need it. Others stop because they do not like the associated side effects. Since many antianxiety medications take several weeks to work, patients may give up before the drug has had a chance to work. Patients are not advised to stop taking their medication without a doctor's approval. Several antianxiety drugs can cause withdrawal symptoms if they are not properly tapered (that is, slowly reduced) under a doctor's supervision.

Alternative Treatments

In addition to psychotherapy and medication, some patients have successfully used alternative treatments to treat panic disorder. Various stress and relaxation techniques, such as muscle relaxation and visualization, can temporarily reduce anxiety and feelings of panic. Using a practiced, controlled breathing technique at the beginning of an attack may also help a patient calm down early and avoid a full-blown attack.

Other techniques such as meditation, yoga, and acupuncture may also help treat panic disorder. These techniques have helped Margaret Finnegan, a writing instructor at California State University–Los Angeles. Finnegan has struggled with panic attacks for years, ever since her daughter was diagnosed with epilepsy. Finnegan has found relief in a style of meditation called Vipassana, which has taught her how to cope with her panic and feel in the moment in order to help prevent panicky thoughts from spiraling out of control. She says:

> Now, when my mind starts to spin out tragedies or dwell on past dramas, I'm less likely to get stuck in them. I wake up. When the stress of parenting a chronically ill child ratchets up, I take solace in the fact that my hardships are like each breath: They evolve. They pass. Nothing lasts forever. My situation hasn't changed. I'm still the mom with the sick kid, and that's hard. But my response to my circumstances has changed.[45]

Yoga can also help with panic disorder. Yoga combines physical poses, breathing exercises, and mindful meditation. Studies suggest that practicing yoga can help reduce heart rate and blood pressure. It may also boost brain chemicals that improve feelings of well-being. Many people practice yoga to reduce stress and anxiety. "Because of its focus on attention to inward states, yoga can help get beneath the surface of anxiety to identify triggers, such as unresolved conflicts or habitual thought patterns,"[46] says Timothy McCall, author of *Yoga as Medicine: The Yogic Prescription for Health and Healing.* Incorporating yoga into a treatment plan can be highly effective for people with panic disorder. "Even a 10-minute daily yoga practice increases stress resilience, and contemplative, relaxation-based practices such as restorative yoga help reduce anxiety and fearfulness,"[47] says Bo Forbes, a clinical psychologist and yoga therapist.

> "Because of its focus on attention to inward states, yoga can help get beneath the surface of anxiety to identify triggers, such as unresolved conflicts or habitual thought patterns."[46]
>
> —Timothy McCall, author of *Yoga as Medicine: The Yogic Prescription for Health and Healing.*

Acupuncture is another alternative way to treat anxiety. Acupuncture is the ancient Chinese practice of inserting needles into the body at specific points to alleviate pain and treat many physical, mental, and emotional conditions. Acupuncture is based on the theory that energy flows through the body and illness occurs when something blocks its flow. The placement of acupuncture needles into certain points on the body is believed to restore proper energy flow. Some practitioners claim that acupuncture can help people with panic disorder by relieving pain and slowing the body's production of stress hormones.

Lifestyle Changes

Making specific lifestyle changes is another good way for panic disorder sufferers to reduce their stress and anxiety, as well as the severity of their panic attacks. Getting regular exercise, eating nutritious food, and ensuring the body is well rested are all ways to improve general

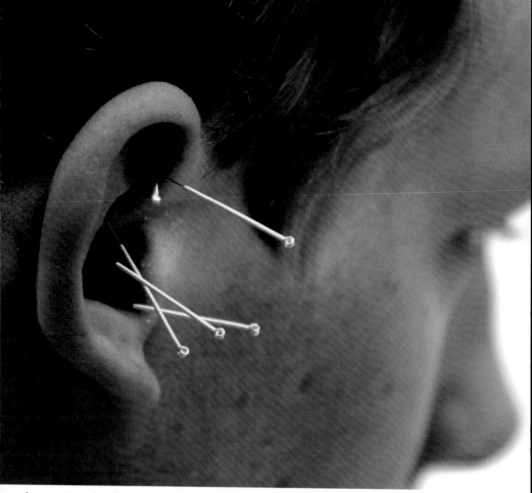

Acupuncture has been used to relieve pain and slow the production of stress hormones in people with panic disorder. This ancient Chinese practice involves the insertion of needles in specific points to reduce pain and treat a variety of conditions.

health and reduce stress. Exercise is particularly useful for reducing stress; physical activity releases chemicals called endorphins into the brain, which improve mood and increase energy.

Being careful to manage stress levels can also reduce the risk and severity of panic disorder. Making sure not to overload one's schedule with activities and commitments can help alleviate a person's stress. Some people find that activities such as music, writing, art, and volunteering help them lower stress levels. Others find that setting aside quiet time each day away from life's distractions allows them to recharge and relax.

Getting support is an important part of learning to manage panic disorder. Support can come in many forms, from many places. Family, friends, doctors, and therapists are all sources of support in a person's life. In addition, people with panic disorder may find comfort in meeting with a group of people who have also been diagnosed with panic disorder. In a support group, they may feel comfortable discussing the symptoms and challenges they face and learning how others have managed the illness.

Being in a support group helped Rita Clark of Lake Forest, California, come to terms with the fact that she has panic disorder. Before seeking treatment and joining the group, Clark hid her panic attacks for twenty years. After being alone with her illness for so long, joining the support group suddenly made Clark feel as if she had a place where she belonged. "I was with people who were all suffering the

Intense Physical Activity Lessens Sensitivity to Anxiety

People who have an intense fear of the symptoms of panic—nausea, racing heart, dizziness, and shortness of breath—may be able to reduce their anxiety by engaging in intense levels of physical activity. Anxiety sensitivity is measured by how much a person fears he or she will be harmed by panic-induced physical sensations. The higher a person's anxiety sensitivity, the greater risk he or she has of developing panic attacks and panic disorder.

In 2011 researchers from Southern Methodist University in Dallas and the University of Vermont in Burlington reported that high-intensity physical activity reduced anxiety sensitivity. In the study, the researchers measured adults' reaction to a panic-related stressor; the adults had no history of panic attacks. After completing a questionnaire that measured physical activity and anxiety sensitivity, the volunteers inhaled air enriched with carbon dioxide, which triggers physical sensations such as nausea, racing heart, dizziness, stomachaches, and shortness of breath. Then they reported their level of anxiety in response to the physical sensations. The researchers found that the participants who had regularly engaged in intense physical activity reacted with lower levels of anxiety to the panic stressor. This could mean that high-intensity activity could be another way for people to reduce or manage their panic disorder.

same thing and were trying to get better," she says. "The therapist and the other people in the group really validated that I was not alone."[48] Even though everyone in the group has different symptoms, Clark says they all feel bonded to each other by a common feeling: being afraid to experience feelings of panic. Group members can relate to her struggles through each step of her recovery and make her feel supported and understood. The group also gives her a place to open up without worrying about what others think.

The High Price of Not Treating

Although panic disorder treatments are more effective the earlier they start, many people delay treatment, and some do not seek treatment at all. According to the NIMH, only 59.1 percent of American adults with panic disorder receive treatment. Many people do not seek treatment because of the stigma mental illness carries. "Stigma is one of the greatest impediments to effective mental health treatment," says Katherine Cowan. "It represses help seeking, creates isolation, and perpetuates the connotations of failure, blame, and shame."[49]

Left untreated, panic disorder can become a severe and isolating illness. Repeated panic attacks can lead to avoidance behaviors, as a person increasingly fears having another attack in public. Over time this behavior can lead to other mental illnesses, such as phobias, depression, and substance abuse, and can significantly impair one's ability to lead a normal life.

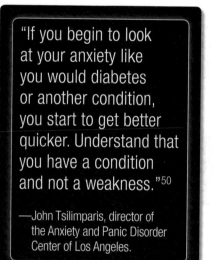

"If you begin to look at your anxiety like you would diabetes or another condition, you start to get better quicker. Understand that you have a condition and not a weakness."[50]

—John Tsilimparis, director of the Anxiety and Panic Disorder Center of Los Angeles.

John Tsilimparis, director of the Anxiety and Panic Disorder Center of Los Angeles, suggests that sufferers who may be reluctant to get treatment think of the disorder as an illness. "If you begin to look at your anxiety like you would diabetes or another condition, you start to get better quicker," he asserts. "Understand that you have a condition and not a weakness."[50]

Karen is one person who struggled with recurring panic attacks before she finally sought treatment; now she feels like an entirely different person. "I used to cry and live in fear, thinking that my life was over," she says. "But now I know my life is just beginning to unfold. So if your heart is beating fast or you feel a little dizzy, remember that it will pass. You, too, can get help. Life is beautiful. Enjoy everything it has to offer and remember to think positively."[51] With appropriate treatment, people living with panic disorder can learn to overcome their fear and panic and can regain control of their lives.

SOURCE NOTES

Introduction: Sudden Terror

1. Lee Kynaston, "Panic Attacks Are Nothing to Be Ashamed Of," *Telegraph*, December 5, 2013. www.telegraph.co.uk.

2. Kynaston, "Panic Attacks Are Nothing to Be Ashamed Of."

3. Priscilla Warner, "How I Overcame a Panic Disorder," *Huffington Post*, September 29, 2011. www.huffingtonpost.com.

4. Rita Zoey Chin, "When Panic Attacks," *Marie Claire*, May 31, 2014. www.marieclaire.com.

5. Quoted in Evan Lambert, "Emma Stone: I Have a History of Panic Attacks," *People*, June 20, 2012. www.people.com.

6. Kynaston, "Panic Attacks Are Nothing to Be Ashamed Of."

Chapter 1: What Is Panic Disorder?

7. Quoted in Catherine O'Brien, "'Anxiety Was My Prison': Jemma Kidd on How She Overcame Her Crippling Panic Attacks," *MailOnline*, January 24, 2011. www.dailymail.co.uk.

8. Quoted in O'Brien, "'Anxiety Was My Prison.'"

9. Lisa T. McElroy, "Worrying Enormously About Small Things," *Slate*, July 18, 2013. www.slate.com.

10. Quoted in Andreas Graven, "Exercise Helps Curb Panic Disorder Symptoms," ScienceNordic, October 30, 2013. http://science nordic.com.

11. McElroy, "Worrying Enormously About Small Things."

12. Traci Neal, "When Panic Attacks," *Catholic Digest*, April 2009, p. 108.

13. Becky, "What It's like to Have Agoraphobia," YoungMinds, May 31, 2012. www.youngminds.org.uk.

14. Quoted in Lily Partland, "'I Fear Going Outside': Living with Agoraphobia," ABC Ballarat, August 21, 2013. www.abc.net.au.

15. Karen Wang, "Meltdown Management: How to Manage and Prevent a Panic Attack," Friendship Circle, December 21, 2011. www.friendshipcircle.org.

16. Wendy Sue Swanson, "How to Ease Your Child's Separation Anxiety," HealthyChildren.org, May 6, 2015. www.healthy children.org.

17. Ashley Nessman, "The Panic Attack That Changed My Life," *Huffington Post*, January 19, 2015. www.huffingtonpost.com.

18. Quoted in Laura Lennie, "One Teen's Struggles with Social Anxiety and Panic Disorders and How She Has Managed to Get Her Life on Track," *Hamilton (ON) Community News*, March 26, 2015. www.hamiltonnews.com.

19. Quoted in Lennie, "One Teen's Struggles with Social Anxiety and Panic Disorders and How She Has Managed to Get Her Life on Track."

Chapter 2: What Causes Panic Disorder?

20. Quoted in Sheryl Kraft, "Menopause and Anxiety: What's the Connection?," HealthyWomen, August 9, 2011. www.healthy women.org.

21. Quoted in Rick Nauert, "Twin Studies Suggest Genetic Risk for Panic Disorder," Psych Central, Retrieved April 16, 2015. http:// psychcentral.com.

22. Quoted in Centre for Genomic Regulation, "Gene Found Responsible for Susceptibility to Panic Disorder," ScienceDaily, November 28, 2013. www.sciencedaily.com.

23. Jieun E. Kim et al., "The Role of the Amygdala in the Pathophysiology of Panic Disorder: Evidence from Neuroimaging Studies," *Biology of Mood & Anxiety Disorders*, November 20, 2012. www .biolmoodanxietydisord.com.

24. Quoted in Medical News Today, "Inhaled Carbon Dioxide Increases Brain Acidity and Evokes Fear Behavior: Study," November 26, 2009. www.news-medical.net.

25. Quoted in Brown University, "Panic Symptoms Increase Steadily, Not Acutely, After Stressful Event," ScienceDaily, June 20, 2011. www.sciencedaily.com.

26. Quoted in Brown University, "Panic Symptoms Increase Steadily, Not Acutely, After Stressful Event."

Chapter 3: What Is It like to Live with Panic Disorder?

27. Neal Sideman, "How I Achieved My Cure of Panic Disorder and Agoraphobia: An Open Letter to Those on the Healing Path," Triumph Over Panic, 2010. www.paniccure.com.

28. Warner, "How I Overcame a Panic Disorder."

29. Quoted in European Society of Cardiology, "Panic Attacks Linked to Higher Risk of Heart Attacks and Heart Disease, Especially in Younger People," ScienceDaily, December 12, 2008. www.sciencedaily.com.

30. Quoted in Michael Timmermann, "Ending the Nightmare," Anxiety and Depression Association of America. www.adaa.org.

31. Kara Baskin, "Panic in Paradise," *Opinionator* (blog), *New York Times*, March 31, 2012. http://opinionator.blogs.nytimes.com.

32. Baskin, "Panic in Paradise."

33. Katherine C. Cowan, "A Journey Through the Labyrinth of Mental Illness," *Phi Delta Kappan*, December 2014/January 2015, p. 14.

34. Quoted in Dina Behrman, "Panic Attacks Almost Ended My TV Career, Says Daybreak's Anna Williamson," *Daily Mail* (London), March 24, 2012. www.dailymail.co.uk.

35. Dan Harris, "How an On-Air Panic Attack Improved My Life," ABC News, February 12, 2014. http://abcnews.go.com.

36. Quoted in Arline Kaplan, "Panic Attacks and Suicide," *Psychiatric Times*, February 12, 2013. www.psychiatrictimes.com.

37. Quoted in Kaplan, "Panic Attacks and Suicide."

38. Quoted in Lindsay Holmes, "5 of the Most Helpful Things You Can Say to Someone with Anxiety," *Huffington Post*, October 16, 2014. www.huffingtonpost.com.

39. Quoted in Lindsay Holmes, "What Not to Do When Someone Is Having a Panic Attack," *Huffington Post*, November 13, 2014. www.huffingtonpost.com.

40. Stacy Gregg, "Now I'm in Control," Anxiety and Depression Association of America. www.adaa.org.

Chapter 4: Can Panic Disorder Be Treated or Cured?

41. Cowan, "A Journey Through the Labyrinth of Mental Illness."

42. Kynaston, "Panic Attacks Are Nothing to Be Ashamed Of."

43. Eric Goodman, "Exposure Therapy for Fear of Panic Attacks," Coastal Center for Anxiety Treatment. http://coastalcenter.org.

44. Quoted in *London Evening Standard*, "Ellie Goulding Opens Up About Panic Attacks and Men," December 4, 2013. www.standard.co.uk.

45. Margaret Finnegan, "My Turn: Don't Panic—Meditation Can Help," *Los Angeles Times*, April 18, 2011. http://articles.latimes.com.

46. Quoted in Jennifer Van Pelt, "Integrating Yoga and Meditation with Anxiety Treatment," *Social Work Today*, May/June 2013. www.socialworktoday.com.

47. Quoted in Van Pelt, "Integrating Yoga and Meditation with Anxiety Treatment."

48. Quoted in Diana Rodriguez, "Getting Support to Manage Anxiety Disorders," EverydayHealth.com, June 2, 2009. www.everydayhealth.com.

49. Cowan, "A Journey Through the Labyrinth of Mental Illness."

50. Quoted in Margarita Tartakovsky, "How to Halt and Minimize Panic Attacks," Psych Central, January 30, 2013. http://psych central.com.

51. Karen, "Achieving Happiness," Anxiety and Depression Association of America. www.adaa.org.

ORGANIZATIONS TO CONTACT

American Academy of Child & Adolescent Psychiatry

3615 Wisconsin Ave. NW
Washington, DC 20016
phone: (202) 966-7300
fax: (202) 966-2891
website: www.aacap.org

The academy is a national professional medical association dedicated to treating and improving the quality of life for children, adolescents, and families affected by mental, behavioral, or developmental disorders.

American Foundation for Suicide Prevention (AFSP)

120 Wall St., 29th Floor
New York, NY 10005
phone: (888) 333-2377
fax: (212) 363-6237
e-mail: info@afsp.org
website: www.afsp.org

The AFSP is the leading national not-for-profit organization dedicated to understanding and preventing suicide through research, education, and advocacy and to reaching out to people with mental disorders and those impacted by suicide.

American Psychiatric Association

1000 Wilson Blvd., Suite 1825
Arlington, VA 22209
phone: (888) 357-7924
e-mail: apa@psych.org
website: www.psychiatry.org

The American Psychiatric Association has more than thirty-eight thousand US and international member physicians working together to ensure humane care and effective treatment for all persons with mental disorders. It publishes many books and journals, including the widely read *American Journal of Psychiatry*.

American Psychological Association

750 First St. NE
Washington, DC 20002-4242
phone: (800) 374-2721
e-mail: public.affairs@apa.org
website: www.apa.org

The American Psychological Association represents more than 148,000 American psychologists, who are professionals who study and treat human behavior. The association's website features information about psychology topics, including panic disorders and links to many publications.

Anxiety Disorders Association of America (ADAA)

8701 Georgia Ave., Suite #412
Silver Spring, MD 20910
phone: (240) 485-1001
fax: (240) 485-1035
website: www.adaa.org

The ADAA is a national nonprofit organization that works to promote the prevention, treatment, and cure of anxiety and other related disorders. It also strives to improve the lives of all those who suffer from them through education, practice, and research. The ADAA website features information, news, and resources for those living with anxiety disorders.

Association for Behavioral and Cognitive Therapies

305 Seventh Ave., 16th Floor
New York, NY 10001

phone: (212) 647-1890
fax: (212) 647-1865
website: www.abct.org

This association represents therapists who provide cognitive behavioral therapy for people who suffer from many types of mental illnesses, including anxiety disorders. The association's website features fact sheets on mental illnesses.

Freedom from Fear

308 Seaview Ave.
Staten Island, NY 10305
phone: (718) 351-1717 ext.20
e-mail: help@freedomfromfear.org
website: www.freedomfromfear.org

Freedom from Fear is a national not-for-profit mental health advocacy association. The organization's mission is to provide a positive impact on the lives of all those affected by anxiety, depression, and related disorders through advocacy, education, research, and community support.

Mental Health America

2000 N. Beauregard St., 6th Floor
Alexandria, VA 22311
phone: (800) 969-6642
fax: (703) 684-5968
website: www.mentalhealthamerica.net

Mental Health America is an advocacy group for people with mental illnesses and their families. Its website features many resources, including fact sheets on anxiety disorders, information on finding support groups, and ways to help support research and funding for mental illnesses.

National Alliance on Mental Illness (NAMI)

3803 N. Fairfax Drive, Suite 100
Arlington, VA 22203
phone: (703) 524-7600

fax: (703) 524-9094
website: www.nami.org

NAMI is an advocacy group for people with mental illnesses and includes local chapters in every state. The alliance offers education programs and services for individuals, family members, health-care providers, and the public. NAMI also serves as a voice in Washington, DC, and statehouses across the country for Americans with mental illness.

National Institute of Mental Health (NIMH)

6001 Executive Blvd.
Bethesda, MD 20892-9663
phone: (866) 615-6464
e-mail: nimhinfo@nih.gov
website: www.nimh.nih.gov

The NIMH is the federal government's chief funding agency for mental health research in America. The institute's website provides fact sheets and information about mental illness, including panic disorders, and the latest science news and research on these illnesses.

FOR FURTHER RESEARCH

Books

Noah Berlatsky, *Mental Illness*. Detroit, MI: Greenhaven, 2013.

Shirley Brinkerhoff, *Anxiety Disorders*. Broomhall, PA: Mason Crest, 2014.

Dale Carlson and Michael Bower, *Out of Order: Young Adult Manual of Mental Illness and Recovery*. Branford, CT: Bick, 2013.

Rudolph Hatfield, *The Everything Guide to Coping with Panic Disorder*. Avon, MA: Adams Media, 2014.

Christopher Willard, *Mindfulness for Teen Anxiety: A Workbook for Overcoming Anxiety at Home, at School, and Everywhere Else*. Oakland, CA: New Harbinger, 2014.

Periodicals

Rita Zoey Chin, "When Panic Attacks," *Marie Claire*, May 31, 2014.

Internet Sources

Beyondblue, "Panic Disorder," 2015. www.beyondblue.org.au/the -facts/anxiety/types-of-anxiety/panic-disorder.

Lee Kynaston, "Panic Attacks Are Nothing to Be Ashamed Of," *Telegraph*, December 5, 2013. www.telegraph.co.uk.

National Alliance on Mental Illness, "Panic Disorder Fact Sheet," February 2013. www2.nami.org/factsheets/panicdisorder_factsheet .pdf.

National Institute of Mental Health, "Panic Disorder: When Fear Overwhelms," 2013. www.nimh.nih.gov/health/publications/panic -disorder-when-fear-overwhelms/index.shtml.

Ashley Nessman, "The Panic Attack That Changed My Life," *Huffington Post*, January 19, 2015. www.huffingtonpost.com.

Websites

Anxieties (www.anxieties.com). This website provides information about anxiety disorders and treatments.

Dana Foundation (www.dana.org). This website provides information about the brain, including research on the brain and mental illness.

Freedom from Fear (www.freedomfromfear.org). This website is an anxiety resource site, providing information about a variety of anxiety disorders and treatment options.

Teen Mental Health (www.teenmentalhealth.org). This website provides information and resources for teens to learn about mental health issues.

INDEX

Note: Boldface page numbers indicate illustrations.

ACCN2 gene, 28
acupuncture, 60, **61**
adolescents. *See* children/
   adolescents
adrenaline. *See* epinephrine
agoraphobia, 16–18, **20**
American Foundation for
   Suicide Prevention, 48
American Psychiatric
   Association, 34
American Psychological
   Association, 25, 51
amygdalae, 28–29
antidepressants, 56–57
Anxiety and Depression
   Association of America
   (ADAA), 9, 18, 47
anxiety/anxiety disorders, 22, 56
   anticipatory, 15–16
   caffeine and, 43
   high-intensity physical activity
      and, 62

Baker, Allison, 49
Baskin, Kara, 42–43
benzodiazepines, 57
beta blockers, 57–59
Biological Psychiatry (journal), 25
Bolton, Donna, 17–18, 19
brain
   biochemistry of, 30–32
   low pH in, 33–34

parts involved in panic
   disorder, 26, 28–30
Brown University, 34
bullying, 32

caffeine, 43
Campbell, Earl, 9
capnometry-assisted respiratory
   therapy (CART) breathing, 55
Centre for Genomic Regulation
   (CRG), 27, 30
children/adolescents, panic
   disorder in, 19–22
Chin, Rita Zoey, 8–9
Clark, Rita, 62–63
cognitive behavioral therapy
   (CBT), 52, 54
cortisol, 33
Cowan, Katherine C., 43, 52, 63
Cowan, Sara, 43, 52

deoxyribonucleic acid (DNA),
   26
*Diagnostic and Statistical Manual
   of Mental Disorders*, 14
diazepam (Valium), 57
Dierssen, Mara, 27
dopamine, 30

elderly patients, panic disorder
   in, 15
epinephrine (adrenaline), 29, 30,
   33, 46, 58
European Society of Cardiology,
   40

PICTURE CREDITS

ABOUT THE AUTHOR

Carla Mooney is the author of many books for young adults and children. She lives in Pittsburgh, Pennsylvania, with her husband and three children.